Guildford
A Walk Through Time

DAVID ROSE & MARTIN GILES

GW00601157

Dragon Enterprises

Gargunnock Books

Published by Gargunnock Books
Woking, Surrey GU21 7PS,
for Dragon Enterprises.

The right of David Rose and Martin Giles of Dragon Enterprises to be identified as the authors of this work has been asserted in accordance with the Copyrights, Designs and Patents Act 1988.

ISBN 978-0-9561723-3-4

Typeset in 9pt on 9.5pt Times.
Typesetting and design by
Dragon Enterprises.
Printed in the UK by
printondemand-worldwide.com

The authors

David Rose

David is a local historian and writer who has lived in Guildford all his life. Until March 2011, he was a senior journalist at the *Surrey Advertiser*. He has a vast collection of vintage photographs of Guildford and the surrounding areas, as well as local history books, directories, pamphlets and all kinds of ephemera including old advertising relating to Guildford. His speciality is modern history, which he calls 'history within living memory'. He regularly gives talks on a number of local history subjects, ranging from his collection of old bottles and bygones to Guildford in the Second World War.

Martin Giles

Martin went to school in Guildford and has lived in the town since 1985, following 10 years' service in the local Queen's Regiment. His family history is deeply rooted in West Surrey and 20th-century history was a regular topic of debate during childhood family meals. Matthew Alexander's photographic books of the town, *Guildford As It Was* and *Vintage Guildford*, were probably the initial spurs to an interest in Guildford's history, in particular, and made him realise how many of the town's old buildings he had witnessed destroyed in the 1960s and 70s. Together with David Rose and others he has given local history presentations and led history walks in St Catherine's and Guildford. He is also the publisher of the St Catherine's Village Website and co-founder, with David Rose, of Dragon Enterprises (see page 88 for further information).

Introduction

WHEREVER you go in Guildford town centre there is a wealth of history all around just waiting to be discovered. There are traces of our Saxon ancestors within the tower of St Mary's Church, while the Normans have provided us with the Great Tower (or keep) in the Castle Grounds. There are medieval remnants too, such as two undercrofts in the High Street. One of them is beneath the Angel Hotel.

The 17th century can be seen in the form of the famous Guildhall clock and Abbot's Hospital – the latter recognised by many as the town's finest building. The facades of some of the High Street's 18th-century town houses can still be glimpsed, albeit from the first floor upwards. What were once the front doors and ground-floor windows of these buildings are now, of course, the entrances to the town's wide range of shops.

The Victorians have certainly left their mark here, with a number of interesting buildings that luckily have survived the ravages of the post-war era of redevelopment. The 1950s and 60s was a time when it was fashionable in towns and cities up and down the country to quickly demolish the old and replace with often rather bland buildings, with apparently no thought as to how they might blend with existing structures in the overall townscape.

In this book we have used a mixture of Edwardian postcard photographs and other early- to mid-20th century views, each one juxtaposed as near as possible with the same scene in 2011, to guide you on a short walk that's less than a mile and a half in length, around the centre of the town. Our text includes instructions to guide you along the route, comparisons to each 'then' and 'now' view, plus snippets of history directly related to each pair of photos. It is advisable to use the pictures themselves to find the exact position for view points.

Of course, if the actual walk does not appeal or is not possible, just find a comfy chair and use the photographs to enjoy a virtual 'Walk Through Time'.

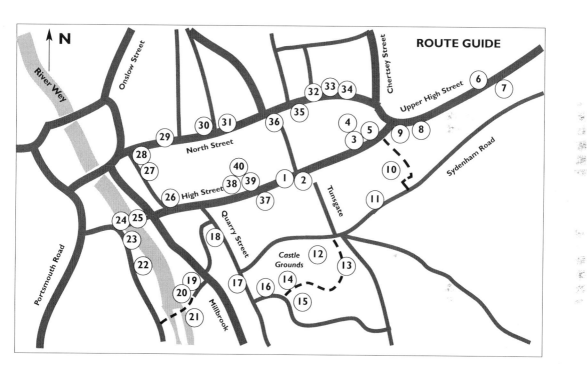

We start in the town centre near the Guildhall, facing east, looking up the High Street. Note the granite setts that are beneath your feet. They were first laid in 1868 and must have been a vast improvement helping horses' hooves grip the road surface while also being easy to hose down, if necessary, after market day. These setts are sometimes incorrectly referred to as cobbles, which are naturally rounded stones. **Now turn to your left and look down Market Street....**

History: The Guildhall has medieval origins. With its projecting clock it is the enduring symbol of Guildford. In earlier times town guilds exercised extensive control over the lives of the town's inhabitants. Until 1626 the front of the Guildhall housed the Corn Market. In 1683, the date displayed on the clock, it was rebuilt in an attractive style showing continental influences. Behind the gallery it housed a council chamber used until 1931 that doubled as a courtroom, where some trials would have led to a sentence of transportation to Australia.

8

Market Street was at one time the site of a very prestigious inn called the Red Lion (on the left). The 17th-century diarist Samuel Pepys stayed there on several occasions. On a journey from Portsmouth to London, Pepys wrote: '...and so to Gilford, where we lay at the Red Lyon, the best inn, and lay in the room the king lately lay in.' **Continue up the High Street, walking on the granite setts if closed to traffic during the daytime, or on the pavement...**

History: Market Street was originally the 'gate' or side passage that ran by the side of the Red Lion Inn. Originally, many or all High Street properties would have had such gates and a few remain e.g. Angel Gate. The Red Lion was once the largest and most prestigious of Guildford's coaching inns. The property to the right was, for at least 400 years, a pub called the Bulls Head. Many lamented the final closing of its doors as a pub in 1988 and since then it has been just another shop.

Pause opposite Guildford House on the left-hand side, opposite Sainsbury's supermarket. You will notice that the High Street contains buildings of a variety of ages and styles. At the time of the Domesday Book in 1086 it is estimated that Guildford had a population of around 800. Most would have lived on or around the High Street. By the 18th century the population was estimated to be about 2,500, taking it 700 years to treble in size! It was the coming of the railway in 1845 that saw Guildford develop rapidly with a continual influx of people. By the 1940s the population had topped 40,000. About 67,000 people live in Guildford today, with the borough's total population being about 130,000. Guildford receives many thousands of visitors each year, and there's always someone taking a photo of the famous Guildhall and clock. In 2011, Guildford's Tourist Information Centre was moved from Tunsgate to Guildford House. The move proved controversial. Some felt the High Street location was ideal, others that it spoiled the carefully restored house. **Guildford House also hosts a wide range of temporary art exhibitions. If open, do go in...**

History: Guildford House was built in 1660 by John Childe, a lawyer and son of a Buckinghamshire gentleman. He was Mayor of Guildford in 1676, 1681 and 1691. On his death in 1701, the house passed to his second son, Leonard, also a lawyer and a town clerk of Guildford. A third generation of the Childe family, Leonard's nephew Charles, had ownership of this impressive town house, but he sold it to a John Martyr in 1736 for £700. The Martyrs were a well known Guildford family and John was an attorney as well as a local magistrate. The house remained in their family for over 100 years. Like other houses fronting the High Street it eventually became a shop. From 1850 to 1878 it was occupied by Frank Apted who ran a brush and turnery business from the building. He later went into partnership with a Mr Bull, a saddler and tent maker. From the early 1900s it became a stationers and bookshop owned by a Mr A. C. Curtis. After being used as a carpet shop for a few years, from 1929 to 1956 it was used as a restaurant, first named Lambert's Tea Room and Grill, and then Nuthalls. In 1959 it was bought by the borough council to house its art collection and opened as a gallery.

Once inside Guildford House, make your way upstairs to the Powell Room that overlooks the High Street. It is named after Alderman Lawrence Powell (1889-1973), who was passionate about the arts and instrumental in Guildford Borough Council's decision to buy Guildford House in 1959 and open it as an art gallery. He was made a freeman of the borough in 1957.

Walk further up the High Street to Abbot's Hospital...

History: Nuthalls was a popular venue for wedding receptions. Many a Guildford couple took advantage of the beautiful carved wooden bannisters on the staircase and the decorative plaster ceiling in the Powell Room as backdrops for their wedding photographs. On a daily basis the restaurant was in the style of a very formal tea shop. Waitresses were dressed like Victorian housemaids complete with cap. Other tea shops at the time included Lyons Corner House and the Corona café, but many regarded Nuthalls as the most elegant.

14

You should now be standing outside the building that is known as Abbot's Hospital. These views were taken from the first-floor bay window of the County Club. Work began on this almshouse in 1619. In 1685 the Duke of Monmouth, who led the Monmouth rebellion, was kept here for one night on his way to his botched and gruesome execution in London.

Move on past the junction with North Street/Chertsey Street and continue to the upper High Street...

History: George Abbot was born in a humble cottage near the Town Bridge. He was educated at the Royal Grammar School, joined the church and rose, through intellectual ability, to become the Archbishop of Canterbury. He decided to create a hospital or almshouse for the poorer and elderly inhabitants of his hometown. It is a fine example of its type, similar in style to the Whitgift Hospital in Croydon, with reflections of Hampton Court and also Oxford and Cambridge college buildings, a style that was actually going out of fashion by the time it was completed.

UPPER HIGH ST., AND GRAMMAR SCHOOL, GUILDFORD.

Cross the road to see this view of the whitewashed Royal Grammar School. Despite being surrounded by shops and restaurants this ancient building, fittingly, still dominates this part of the upper High Street. The modern part of the school stands opposite. Note the royal coat of arms and date above the door in the centre of the building.

Re-cross and walk to Somerset House with its characteristic steps and railings...

History: The Royal Grammar School was founded with a legacy from a London grocer, Richard Beckingham, in the early 1500s to teach 30 of the town's poorest boys. It was re-endowed by Edward VI in 1552 and the school-house, which has a rare chained library, was built between 1557 and 1586. Its fortunes have waxed and waned. In 1889 there were just six pupils. In the 1970s, with the demise of the 11-plus in Surrey, the school became an independent grammar school. Past pupils include Terry Jones of Monty Python fame and cricketer Bob Willis.

Guildford, High Street.

Note how narrow this part of the upper High Street was when the picture postcard view was taken in the early 1900s. This was once known as Spittle Street, derived from the word 'hospital' of which a St Thomas' Hospital was once located further along near Epsom Road. It closed in the mid 1850s. The council was eventually persuaded to change the name of the road to something less crude! **Now head back to the junction of High Street and Chertsey Street...**

History: The Grade I listed Somerset House (seen to the right), was built in about 1700 by Charles Seymour, the sixth Duke of Somerset, as a stop over on his frequent journeys between London and his Petworth House estate. He avoided local taxes by constructing it just outside the town boundary of the time. Architectural critics Nairn and Pevsner have noted: 'Heavy handsome ironwork and flight of stone steps to front door, undoubtedly original.' Many feel the current shop fronts deface what is one of Guildford's finest pieces of architecture.

Pause some 50 yards before the road junction and compare the past and present views. The older picture dates to about 1910 and you can see that a line of buildings once extended out further from the High Street. The large white building was the Ram Inn. The shops on the right were replaced by the current buildings in the 1960s. **Make your way to the George Abbot statue just before Holy Trinity Church...**

History: The medieval streets of Guildford were, of course, not designed for motor vehicles. As traffic increased 'choke points' such as the narrow opening (just 13 feet wide) to the High Street became more and more of an inconvenience. The Ram Inn seems to have dated from the second half of the 18th century and included, according to an 1847 description, a covered skittle alley, well and piggery. Despite the traffic relief offered, its destruction in 1913 was not universally welcomed.

Notice in the early 1900s view the large pair of spectacles on Horstmanns' opticians to the left of the church. One of the buildings on the right was at that time the High Street's post office. The only one in the town centre today has, in fact, in recent times been relocated just around the corner from here at the top of North Street. The Three Pigeons pub back then offered accommodation. **Take the path to the left of the church and walk up beside the churchyard...**

History: Despite George Abbot's status as Guildford's most famous son, it was only in 1995 that a statue was erected to him. Fittingly, it stands at the top of the High Street near the almshouse he created and Holy Trinity Church where his tomb is. His brother Maurice became Lord Mayor of London. Sons of a cloth worker, their origins lay in a humble cottage at the bottom of the High Street. Holy Trinity is Surrey's only large 18th-century church and the architecture has been described as 'handsome and pedestrian at the same time'.

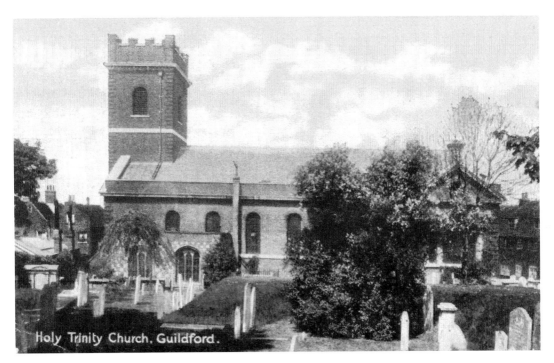

Holy Trinity Church, Guildford.

24

At the top of the path turn right and stop outside the entrance to the Royal Oak pub. The most striking feature is how much the trees have filled in around the churchyard. Lining up today's view exactly with the older one would not have resulted in a pleasing image, so we stood a short distance to the left from the position adopted by the postcard photographer of about 100 years ago. **Continue past the pub, turn left and leave the churchyard...**

History: A medieval church stood on this site until 1740 when its tower collapsed whilst 'improvements' were being carried out. Most of the old church was destroyed. Miraculously, George Abbot's tomb survived, as did the Weston Chapel, its chalk and flint chequerboard walls are easily identified. In the middle of the graveyard is an L-shaped mound. This is not, as many believe, a mass grave for victims of the Black Death but simply the enturfed rubble from the original church. The original rectory became the Royal Oak pub in about 1870.

Cross Sydenham Road and view the Castle Car Park. As the volume of motor traffic increased during the 1950s, this area was cleared and used as a car park. In 1963 a multi-storey car park was built here, considered by many as a monstrosity! However, the top level did offer great views of the town. It became unsafe in the 1990s and was rebuilt with a car park building more pleasing on the eye.

Walk on to the entrance of the Castle Grounds, opposite Tunsgate...

History: The two roads running parallel to the High Street were originally called Lower Back Side (now North Street) and Upper Back Side. This later became South Street at its western end, with the eastern end being named Sydenham Road after a 17th-century physician. The whole of the road had become Sydenham Road by the 1960s. The old photo shows what was the Queens Head pub – a lovely tile-hung building that did not escape the demolition man's ball and chain when this part of the town was redeveloped in the late 1950s.

(12)

Enter the Castle Grounds, walk past the war memorial, keep right of the bowling green and then turn around to see this view.

The house behind the memorial is built on the site of a former dwelling that was used by the head gardener. Up until 1887 the house had been a pub, the Bowling Green Inn. **Walk back past the war memorial, going around the other side of the bowling green to get an excellent view of the castle keep...**

History: Guildford lost 492 men in the Great War and was determined to remember their sacrifice in the 'war to end all wars'. Some names were removed from the memorial, erected in 1920, on discovery that the men had, in fact, survived! The design for the memorial was decided by competition. It was won by local architect Frederick Hodgson and judged by none other than the famous designer of the Cenotaph, Sir Edwin Lutyens. The central plinth for those who died in the Second World War was only erected in 1995.

The bowling green, which perhaps enjoys one of the most attractive settings in the region, has been here since at least the 1660s. In Victorian times the grounds were opened at night and lit by fairy lamps. Incredibly, one head gardener organised tightrope walking and firework displays. **Walk around the bowling green. Follow a path that takes you through a short tunnel. Turn left, and with the castle on your right, follow the path as it then bears right...**

History: We might look with some affection at the Norman castle these days as one of the most historic buildings in Guildford. However, Guildfordians who may have been used as forced labour in its construction in the century that followed the Conquest probably hated it. It was built to subjugate the town, part of a strategy to allow the relatively small number of Normans to keep control of a resentful population. The height of the keep was later increased: the shape of the original crenallations is discernable in the recent protective rendering.

Castle Grounds   Guildford

You should now be standing beside an area of grass on your left and an ornamental pond to your right. It is known as Peak's Pond, named after Henry Peak, a borough surveyor from the 19th century, who supervised the landscaping of the Castle Grounds. The pond is, in fact, smaller these days, and does not have a fountain, but in recent years has benefited from some renovation.

Turn around and leave the Castle Grounds by the exit facing you into Castle Hill...

History: The motte and bailey layout of the castle can be best appreciated from the gardens which are largely contained within the deep ditch cut to separate and heighten the end of the spur on which the 'Great Tower' was built. Because much of the mound comprised of spoil from the ditch, the weight of the keep is largely taken by the east wall, the foundations of which rest in the chalk bedrock. In 1885, Guildford Corporation bought the castle grounds. They rejected the idea of demolishing the 'ugly ruin' and laid out the moat as a public garden.

The second large house uphill to the left is The Chestnuts. This house was leased by the Rev Charles Lutwidge Dodgson (also known as Lewis Carroll, the writer of the Alice books) for his six unmarried sisters to live in. The house was built in 1862 and the Dodgson sisters came to live there in 1868 after the death of their father, who was the Archdeacon of Richmond and Canon of Ripon in Yorkshire. Guildford was an ideal location for the Dodgson sisters – half-way between their brother's home in Oxford and the south coast resorts and the Isle of Wight. They also had other relatives living in the south of England. These well-off sisters did not have to work, but kept themselves busy in the parish with, for example, organising mothers' meetings, tea parties and Sunday school treats for local children.

Move down Castle Hill – a one-way street that can be busy with traffic – pause before you reach the stone arch…

History: The Rev Charles Lutwidge Dodgson was an Oxford don. His book, *Alice's Adventures in Wonderland*, was published in 1865. He was a regular visitor to Guildford, staying with his sisters at The Chestnuts, especially at Christmas time. He sometimes preached at St Mary's Church in Quarry Street. He had been ordained deacon in 1861, but did not advance to priesthood, partly because he was afflicted with a stammer. In Guildford he had an active social life and was good friends with his elderly next-door-neighbour Miss Haydon. His death here was sudden and a shock. He took ill with flu, it went to his chest and he never recovered. Although he was a famous writer at the time, his funeral was poorly attended. He lies buried in the Mount Cemetery. His sisters placed a simple white cross on his grave with the words 'Charles Lutwidge Dodgson (Lewis Carroll) fell asleep January 14th, 1898'.

Castle Arch & Museum, Guildford.

The fine house to your right is the home of the Surrey Archeological Society and Guildford Museum. This picturesque town house dates back to the 17th century. However, note in the old picture postcard how the buildings to the right-hand side then had windows and appear to have been separate cottages.

Take care when passing through the stone arch as the pavement is very narrow, then turn right...

History: Castle Arch is thought to have been built by John of Gloucester, Henry III's master mason. It has grooves for a portcullis, although the wall here is not the stoutest. Presumably, defence was not top of the agenda when the royal palace was being developed. The arch was probably the main entrance to the castle. In 1978 a large lorry crashed into it causing extensive damage. It was repaired with clunch chalk taken from the same nearby chalk caverns as used during the original construction but now closed for safety reasons.

You are now in Quarry Street. Pause for this view before continuing towards the town centre.

Quarry Street takes its name from the chalk quarry adjacent to the River Wey beside the Shalford Road. What is now the restaurant on the corner of Castle Street was, in the early 19th century, the Guildford Dispensary, a forerunner of the Royal Surrey County Hospital. **Continue past the Kings Head pub, and walk on with St Mary's Church on your left...**

History: Amazingly, until the 1960s this was a main road carrying all the traffic from the town towards Horsham and Brighton. Despite that, children played in the street until the early 20th century, only interrupting their games to allow the passage of occasional vehicles. The Surrey Archeological Society moved into Castle Arch in 1898. In 1911, a purpose-built gallery with a glass roof was added and opened as Guildford Museum. The Muniment Room, also located here, moved to the Surrey History Centre in Woking when it opened in 1999.

Guildford
Quarry Street
and
St. Mary's Church

Pause just past the church and turn to see this view. At the time of writing (2011) the church was undergoing much renovation including re-pointing the stonework and replacing roof tiles. Smoke from the Norman raid on Shalford in 1066 may have been first observed from the top of the tower of St Mary's Church, warning inhabitants of the invasion. **Cross the road carefully, go back towards the church and walk down Mill Lane to Millbrook (the A281)...**

History: The church tower is Saxon and Guildford's oldest building. The church remains structurally much as it was in its heyday during the reign of Henry III, who, with other Plantagenet kings, would have worshiped here. The sisters of the Rev Charles Lutwidge Dodgson (Lewis Carroll) are said to have donated the brass cross on the altar. It is rumoured that George IV had a section of the chancel that stuck out into the road removed in 1825. It was so that his carriage could pass that way through Guildford, en route between Windsor and Brighton.

At the foot of Mill Lane cross Millbrook via the pedestrian crossing and make your way towards the Yvonne Arnaud Theatre. Seen here is an unusual view of the foundations being laid for the theatre back in 1963. It was taken from an upper room of the Town Mill. We have been fortunate to have been given permission by the theatre to take the view today from the same spot. **When in front of the theatre turn around and look back to Millbrook...**

History: The Yvonne Arnaud Theatre is named after a French actress who lived in Guildford. Its shape is constrained by the small site it sits upon. Vanessa Redgrave laid the foundation stone, and in 1965 its first production, *A Month In The Country,* starred the world famous actors Michael Redgrave and Ingmar Bergman. The theatre seats 590, but has a stage almost as large as the London palladium which seats 2,500. The old Town Mill, next door, has been utilised as a studio theatre. It also contains the theatre's extensive costume department.

MILL & CHURCH, GUILDFORD.

44

The Town Mill dominates the view today as it did about 100 years ago.

In the old photograph the tower of St Mary's Church can be seen – trees hide it today. Also note the other buildings now long gone. The one with a pitched roof and semi-circular window was at one time a mortuary.

Turning around once again, continue by taking the footpath that goes past the left-hand side of the Yvonne Arnaud Theatre, past the stage door...

History: There are indications that the river was already being managed by the Saxons, to provide headwater for the mills in the town, before the Norman Conquest. With the introduction of the woollen industry by Cistercian monks, some mills were used in the 'fulling' process to rid the raw wool of lanolin. Guildford contributed fully to the wool trade, which became one of England's most important industries in the Middle Ages. It is believed the reputation of the locally produced 'Guildford Blue' cloth was ruined by over-stretching during the drying process.

Approach to Mill Mead, Guildford.

Stop before the first footbridge beside Millmead Lock to compare these views. The old postcard view was actually taken from a position that is now a narrow piece of ground at the back of the theatre. Tree growth beside the river bank currently obliterates that same view, so we have moved slightly to the left for today's picture. **Continue on and go over the second footbridge and turn right into Millmead and walk on the path beside the river...**

History: Originally, Guildford's riverside sites were used primarily by local industry and businesses such as Moon's timber yard and Filmer & Mason's iron foundry, which made use of river barges for transportation. Unfortunately, the closeness of the waterway backfired when in 1900 the river flooded and timber was washed down to the nearby Town Bridge, jamming under the arches. This caused immense pressure to be put on the medieval structure which eventually partially collapsed.

With the Britannia pub on your left continue past the parking bays and pause where the road narrows. The older view dates from the 1950s and shows the buildings of timber merchants John Moon & Son not long before they relocated to Walnut Tree Close. The department store Plummers opened on the site in the mid-1960s, and today, of course, it is Debenhams. **Now continue along the towpath close to the river and pause beside the White House pub...**

History: Making the River Wey navigable with 12 locks, from the Thames to Guildford, in 1653 was the first major step in opening up trading routes from the town. It was the brainchild of Sir Richard Weston of Sutton Place who had seen the benefits of canals while in Holland. The navigation was continued up to Godalming in 1764. Coal, corn, gunpowder (from Chilworth), timber, lime and even cases of bottled ginger beer were transported. The town charged 1d for every ton. The last commercial barge journey was made in 1969.

The Town Bridge is now in front of you.

The older photograph dates to about the 1890s – note the buildings beyond the bridge. Back then there were a number of traders hereabouts with Henry Martin's premises visible. He had a boat hire business and sold fishing tackle. In 1903 the business was taken over by Harry How who offered 'sumptuous hampers' to boaters.

Follow the path round to the bridge and walk across it...

History: It is commonly accepted that Guildford gets its name from the 'Golden' (most probably from the yellow sand that formed the river bed) ford, situated at the point that the River Wey cuts through the North Downs. Permanent settlement around the ford, the focal point of Guildford's origin, commenced in Saxon times, around the year 500. In the Middle Ages a bridge was constructed, presumably to allow travellers to keep dry, but the ford remained alongside until the 1760s when the river was dredged to make it navigable to Godalming.

St. Nicholas Church, Guildford.

When you are about two-thirds of the way across the Town Bridge, stop and turn around.

Here is a view that would appear to have changed little. Although St Nicolas' Church is much the same, opposite was once Crooke's brewery and also the Commercial Hotel (now a car park). Where the White House pub is today was once the premises and yard of John Moon & Son's stonemasonry business.

Turn around and continue across the bridge...

History: Some believe that the site on which St Nicolas' Church stands, beside the ancient ford, might have been where the first church in Guildford was built. Its riverside siting has made it subject to periodic damage by floods. The height of the 1968 floodwater is marked on the side of the church. The medieval church was replaced in 1836, but poor design and construction meant that by 1871 it had to be replaced again. A plan to move the church to higher ground by the Portsmouth Road was resisted by parishioners and the current church was completed in 1875.

LOWER HIGH STREET, GUILDFORD.

1917 LLOYD, ALBURY.

You will now see the High Street rising in front of you on the opposite side of Millbrook. In the old postcard view notice the jumble of shops that once reached down to the bridge. Now the busy A281 sweeps through. One of the shops on the right-hand side must have been a butcher's, as there is a sign advertising 'Canterbury Lamb'.
Using the pedestrian crossing, cross the road. Then go over the crossing at the foot of High Street...

History: Originally the Saxon settlement that was 'Gyldeford' would have comprised of this single street ascending the hill from the old ford. The street itself is on the route of what might be a primeval east-west trackway that followed the chalk ridge that forms the North Downs. It was not until 1868 that it was properly paved. In Victorian times the High Street had 30 public houses. Now there is just one, the Three Pigeons at the top of the street.

You will now be facing the pedestrianised and recently revamped Friary Street. The vintage photograph dates back to 1935 when the town was celebrating the silver jubilee of George V. Not only was the High Street festooned with flags and bunting, but so were side streets such as this one. The vehicle has come to a halt in front of a STOP sign painted on the road. Traffic lights can be seen to the left. **Walk on through Friary Street...**

History: Behind the buildings on the side of Friary Street nearest to the river was the town wharf, in operation from 1653 to 1968, and the offices of the Wey Navigations. There is no trace of it today, but it would have once been a bustling place with carts coming and going from an entrance in Friary Street. Four generations of the Stevens family were connected with the waterway. By the 1890s, the family had eight barges and finally gained complete ownership of it by 1902. The Wey Navigations are now in the safe hands of the National Trust.

Continue until you reach the junction with Onslow Street and look back. The older view was taken when Guildford was hit by flooding in 1968. The date is likely to be on Monday or Tuesday, September 15 or 16, when the water was at its highest. In some places in the town it reached six feet. Being so close to the river this part of the town suffered the most. Now turn around and look in the other direction towards the Friary shopping centre...

History: This was once a busy street with traffic going in both directions. It even had its own petrol station, operated by Court & Smith, who are listed in the 1955 edition of Kelly's Directory of Guildford and Godalming as motor car agents, garage and engineers. They were about half-way down on the river side of the street. Dairymen Lymposs & Smee were also here and at this end on the right was a once well known Guildford firm, Fogwills Ltd – coal, corn and seed merchants. The street was re-developed and pedestrianised in the early 1970s.

The Weighing Bridge. Guildford

Much has changed here.
In the foreground of the picture postcard of about 100 years ago we see a public weighbridge and hut for its attendant. On top of the hut is a rather grand gas lamp! To its right is a road sign – the design of which was standard at the time. Beyond can be seen the buildings occupied by the removals firm Pickfords, which remained there until the site was redeveloped in the 1970s.
Now proceed up North Street...

History: In 1274 Prince Henry, son of Edward I, died aged just seven and a Dominican friary was founded here, the following year, in his memory. From this friary the Friary Centre and before it the Friary Brewery obtained their names. Rodboro buildings (to the left) are thought to be the first purpose-built car factory in the UK. They were built by the Dennis brothers who moved to Guildford from Devon in 1895. They started out by making bicycles but saw that the future was in motor vehicles. John Dennis is thought to have committed the first motoring offence in Guildford when he rode a motorised tricycle up the High Street at furious speed.

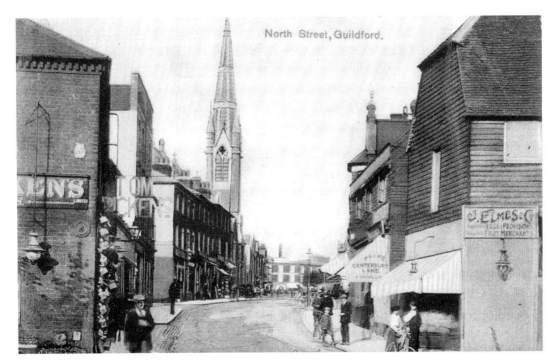

North Street, Guildford.

Pause before the junction with Commercial Road bus station on your left.

Unlike the High Street, much of North Street has changed over the last century. The spire of what was Guildford Methodist Church is clearly seen in the old picture postcard. There's yet another butcher selling lamb from Canterbury! In addition, there is a grocer J. Elmes & Co, and Tom Picken's hardware store. **Carry on up North Street a short distance...**

History: The Friary brewery once dominated the scene to the left of here and could literally be smelt by the aroma of malted barley that emitted from it. By the 1900s it was well established under the ownership of Charles Hoskins-Master and known as the Friary, Holroyd & Healy's Brewery. A merger saw it become Friary Meux in 1956, and by the time it was bought out by Allied Breweries in 1963, it owned 672 pubs across the south of England. The last brew took place in 1969 before the brewery was pulled down and the site redeveloped.

Pause when you reach the junction with Woodbridge Road. Here again is a scene that has changed so much – particularly the buildings at this end of Woodbridge Road, most of which look like they were houses. The vintage photo must date back to the 1880s at least. The only buildings that appear to be recognisable are those on the right-hand side going up North Street.

Continue on the right-hand side of North Street...

History: North Street was once called Lower Back Side as it was delineated by the rear boundaries of the High Street houses' back yards. The street was mentioned in a 1500s court case when a witness stated that it was in this area that in his youth the boys played at 'crekett'. Here we see Guildford's fire brigade with the tender still horse drawn. Later they were equipped with locally produced Dennis fire engines, and in the years following the Great War these were constructed with many parts that had originally been produced for army lorries.

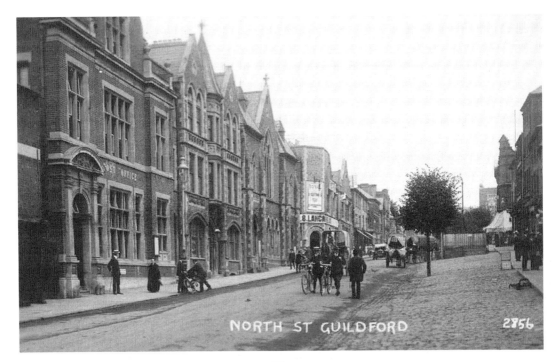

NORTH ST GUILDFORD

2756

When you have passed Swan Lane on your right pause and look across to the other side of North Street.

In the earlier view on the immediate left you can see what was then the town's main post office. Further up you can see a sign and advertisement on the building that in 1912 became the Theatre Royal – originally part of the County and Borough Halls. All fine buildings that perhaps should never have been demolished. **Continue up North Street...**

History: The County and Borough Halls were built of local Bargate stone in 1861 and served the town well for many years as a venue for public events and meetings. The building was also used for the county assizes and petty sessions, with cells in the basements for those prisoners on trial. As well as later being the home of the Theatre Royal, Guildford Co-operative Society was also once based there. On the opposite corner of Leapale Road, at its junction with North Street, once stood the town's Congregational Church, built and opened in 1863.

Halt when you are roughly opposite the junction with Ward Street that is on the opposite side of the road. The older picture dates to the late 1940s. There was a bus stop here back then, just as there is today. The advert on the back of the bus is for Bluecol antifreeze – a brand that was introduced in 1937. A new tree is an unusual addition to today's streetscape. **Remain in the same position and look across to the building that today is topped with a clock tower...**

History: House furnisher Pimm Son & Co Ltd, occupied a large group of buildings at the top of North Street adjoining Chertsey Street. The business was founded by William Pimm in 1835 and also operated one of the town's first estate agents. In the town's official guide book for 1957, Pimms advertised its services as 'specialists in complete house furniture and furnishings, large removal and warehouse department, expert curtain and loose cover makers'. It also offered a funeral service, supplying its own coffins.

The building you are looking at was once Guildford's fire station. The three vehicles seen here in this view from about the 1920s all have the Dennis motor manufacturer's badge on them. They were made in Guildford at the firm's large factory at Woodbridge. By this time, Dennis Bros was back into production of its specialist vehicles after making lorries for the army during the First World War.
Now look at the building to the right, once a pub...

History: Fire was a constant threat in timber-framed buildings with open fires and candles, so having an effective fire brigade was important. In 1871, the part-time Guildford firemen were criticised for stopping at the Prince Albert pub for a drink on the way to tackle a fire at Stoke Mill. However, they were probably just waiting for other members of their crew to muster. The following year this new fire station in North Street was completed. It remained in use until 1937 when a new station was built at Ladymead, the old station serving since as public conveniences.

Looking at this building today, it is hard to imagine that it was the site of a violent and shocking terrorist attack in the 1970s. However, the building has a long history. Part of it was once a barn dating back to the late 17th century. It probably became the Horse and Groom pub in the early 19th century, when there was another pub next to it called the Maltman and Shovel.

Retrace your steps and head back down North Street...

History: At 8.30pm on October 5, 1974, the Horse and Groom in North Street was one of two Guildford pubs bombed by the IRA. Five people were killed and 65 injured. All the pubs in the town were evacuated. In 1975 three men and a young woman were convicted of the bombings and given life sentences, but in 1989 the convictions of the so called 'Guildford Four' were declared a miscarriage of justice and they were released. The story was later made into a film – *In The Name Of The Father*. No one else has been tried for the crime. A memorial to those killed can be found in the public garden opposite.

Pause just before you reach the junction with Market Street on your left. In the postcard view, the spire of Guildford Methodist Church (demolished 1974) once again stands out. The horse-drawn wagon turning out of Leapale Road is from the brewer Savill & Co, which was based in Shalford at Broadmead, near today's Parrot pub. The buildings on the north side of the street today are hardly pleasing on the eye. **Turn to face Market Street...**

History: North Street's popular street market, that takes place every Friday and Saturday, goes back to 1865 when the cattle market moved here from the High Street. Fruit and vegetables were also sold back then, but in 1896 the market moved to a new site in Woodbridge Road. In 1919 a market was re-established for local people to sell off surplus produce they had grown on their allotments. By the 1930s traders were coming from further afield selling jewellery, china, sweets and chocolate. Back then the market continued late into Saturday nights.

Look up Market Street, which at the time of the older photo was open to traffic both ways.

This is a photograph believed to date back to the town's celebrations of George VI's coronation in 1937. As can be seen from this night view, electric lights were strung up as part of the decorations. With the Second World War but a couple of years away, it wasn't long before the town was plunged into darkness during the wartime blackout.

Walk up Market Street...

History: The shop sign on the building on the left of the older photograph reads 'Gammons Ltd'. This was a family run store established in 1878. By the 1950s it proudly boasted: 'In addition to the fine department for men's outfitting and women's wear, there are those for footwear, millinery, hosiery, haberdashery, hardware, toys and furniture, but perhaps the high repute of Gammons is due in great measure to the large and comprehensive stocks of piece goods, the material sold by the yard in the furnishing and dress departments.'

High Street, Guildford.

Turn right into the High Street and walk down a short way.

The older view seems to date from not long before the First World War. There are a few motor vehicles in the scene, but cycling into town appears to have been popular at the time! Note the building with a large window reflecting the one opposite. A sign above reveals it was occupied by an upholsterer at the time. The sundial above is still there today. **Continue down a little further...**

History: The range and types of shops in the High Street are always changing. Once, it was full of local traders such as W. E. White's department store, Hardy's outfitters, and Holden's the high-class grocers. Forty years ago, some bemoaned the town was full of shoe shops and building societies. Small tea shops and cafés, including the Astolat Tea Rooms and Boxers, had closed, with the remaining choice being cafés such as those in Woolworths or Harvey's department store. National chain stores dominate today, with a plethora of mobile phone shops.

80

Pause when you are opposite the Angel Hotel.

Some of the pedestrians appear as just blurs in the older view that dates from the 1930s. Presumably the postcard photographer used a slow shutter speed on the camera. To the right of the Angel can be seen Charles Holden – Guildford's upmarket grocery stores. Marks & Spencer once occupied the building to the left of the hotel.

Now cross over the road...

History: The Angel Hotel is now the only surviving example of the numerous coaching inns that were once on Guildford High Street. It probably started life as a timber-framed house. In the 13th century an undercroft (not a crypt) was constructed which might have been used as a store or as a shop. Guildford's market was originally held on the High Street and from 1345 it included a fish cross (where fish was sold) just by the spot where the Angel now stands. Although the first written evidence of its use as an inn is from 1606, it has probably been one since the 1500s. The building was sold in 1527 for £10.

Take a look at the Angel Hotel Yard.

Visitors who came by car to stay at the hotel in the 1930s would have been put out if there hadn't been a parking space for them! However, the official town guide at about this time was proudly proclaiming that Guildford had three large public car parks – all near the High Street.

Now why not pop into the Angel Hotel – you might like some refreshments at the end of your walk...

History: In common with the other houses on the High Street a side passage or 'gate' ran down the side of the Angel to the town ditch where North Street now is. The gate was expanded making it suitable to facilitate the servicing of the London to Portsmouth coaches. Originally, before the roads were improved in the 1700s, travellers often broke their journey in Guildford, which was roughly half way. Later, when the road was 'turnpiked', the journey time was reduced to nine hours. Stops were still required to change horses and for meals.

Angel Hotel, Guildford,
Surrey Trust House.

'Phone. Guildford 287.

Pause in the lounge area and compare it to about 90-odd years ago.

Gone are the stags' antlers, the other fancy decorations on the walls and the elaborate plant holders. The room has been opened out to the right, but one prominent feature remains – the delightful clock by the stairs. Bearing a date of 1688, it may be a 'parliamentary clock' – a relic from the coaching era when there was a tax on pocket watches.

We hope you enjoyed your walk around Guildford.

History: In 1636 after it had been largely rebuilt, The Angel was described as one of Guildford's 'Very faire innes' and in 1707 it was seen fit to be the venue for a feast for the Mayor and Approved Men. The prominent clock in the lounge would have been important to staff and guests alike as they awaited the arrival of the scheduled coach services, much like a station clock today. Of course, the advent of railway travel had a major detrimental impact on trade and in 1906 an advert included the statement: 'Flys to meet the trains if required.'

Thanks and acknowledgments

The authors would like to thank: Councillor Terence Patrick for a photo of the interior of Guildford House from the Patrick Collection; Alderman Bernard Parke and the County Club for allowing us to take a photo of Abbot's Hospital from a bay window on the club's first floor; Tommy Daniel and the store H&M for the opportunity of taking the photo of the Angel Hotel from the store's first floor window; Isabel Kay, operations assistant and funding officer at the Yvonne Arnaud Theatre, for permission to take a photo of the theatre from the top floor of the adjacent mill building; Michelle Lassiter at the Angel Hotel for permission to take a photograph inside the hotel; the Castle Green Bowling Club and member Ann Bailey; John Gilbert of Gargunnock Books; and Diana Roberts, tourism, marketing and development manager at Guildford Borough Council, for advice on the idea of this book. There are many others who have given verbal encouragement and support including our long-suffering wives, Helen and Fiona; and Martin's son Tom, who has, once again, been invaluable in proof reading the text and also for taking the photo of the authors standing beside the Great Tower (otherwise known as the Keep) in the Castle Grounds. We are very grateful to all of them.

Bibliography and further reading

Books:

Alexander, M. A. *Guildford A Short History*. 1986. Ammonite Books.

Alexander, M. A. *Guildford As It Was*. 1978. Hendon Publishing Company.

Alexander, M. A. *Vintage Guildford*. 1981. Hendon Publishing Company.

Chamberlin, E. R. *Guildford A Biography*. 1970. Macmillan.

Chamberlin, E. R. *Guildford A History & Celebration*. 2004. Ottakar's.

Collyer, G. R. Rose, D. *Images of Guildford*. 1998. Breedon Books.

Hutchinson P. *Guildford (Images of England)*. 2006 The History Press.

Rose, D. *Memory Lane Guildford & District*. 2000. Breedon Books.

Rose, D. *Guildford Our Town – Uncovering The Stories Behind The Facts*. 2001. Breedon Books.

Rose, D. Parke, B. *Guildford Remember When*. 2007. Breedon Books.

Rose, D. Parke, B. *Guildford Through Time*. 2009. Amberley Publishing.

Sturley, Mark. *The Breweries And Public Houses of Guildford*. 1990. Charles W. Traylen.

Williamson, D. *Kings & Queens of Britain*. 1991. Promotional Reprint Company.

Williamson, G. C. *Guildford Charities*. 1931. The Corporation of Guildford.

Other sources:

Guidebook. *Lewis Carroll in Guildford*. 1989. Guildford Borough Council.

Guidebook. *Guildford House Gallery Guide*. 2006. Guildford Borough Council.

Surrey Advertiser. Various editions of its history column, *From the Archives*. 1998-2010. Edited by David Rose.

White, V. Note on Maurice Abbot. 2011.

Wikipedia.

Dragon Enterprises
including books, guided walks, talks and website

Dragon Enterprises, run by Martin Giles and David Rose, is a local business based around Guildford's history, local news and local events, including the following:

Books: other titles available: *St Catherine's Guildford – A Walk Through Time* – an historic tour of a village steeped in history and along a section of the picturesque River Wey, all within walking distance of Guildford town centre. Paperback, £5.99. To order copies, see details below.

Walks: Guided local history walks around Guildford town centre and St Catherine's Village, followed by a PowerPoint presentation of vintage photographs. See website for updates.

Talks: A wide range of local history topics are offered which can be designed to suit various venues, audiences and time slots.

Website: The expanding St Catherine's Village website contains local news and information, plus Through Time – a section devoted to the local history and nostalgia of West Surrey and beyond. Go to st-caths-web.co.uk, or call Martin Giles on 01483 537551. Email: mgilesdragon@gmail.com, or David Rose on 01483 838960. Email: drosedragon@gmail.com